Black inventors

Volume 1

Marie Van Brittan Brown 2

Lewis Howard Latimer 4

Alice H. Parker 6

Granville Woods 8

Dr. Patricia E. Bath 10

Percy Lavon Julian 12

Valerie Thomas 14

Garrett Augustus Morgan 16

Dr. Shirley Jackson, PHD 18

Alexander Miles 20

Dr. Gladys West, PHD 22

Copyright © December 2023 by Oyaka Eboumbou

All rights reserved.

No portion of this book may be reproduced in any form without written permission from the publisher or author, except as permitted by Canada copyright law.

Cover by Oyaka Eboumbou

Illustrations by Oyaka Eboumbou

Marie Van Brittan Brown

Born: October 30, 1922, Jamaica, Queens, New York, U.S.
Died: February 2, 1999, Jamaica, Queens, New York, U.S.
Major Invention: home security system

Naissance : 30 Octobre 1922, Jamaica Queens, New York, U.S.
Décès : 2 Février, 1999, Jamaica, Queens, New York, U.S.
Invention Majeure : System de sécurité résidentielle avec caméra.

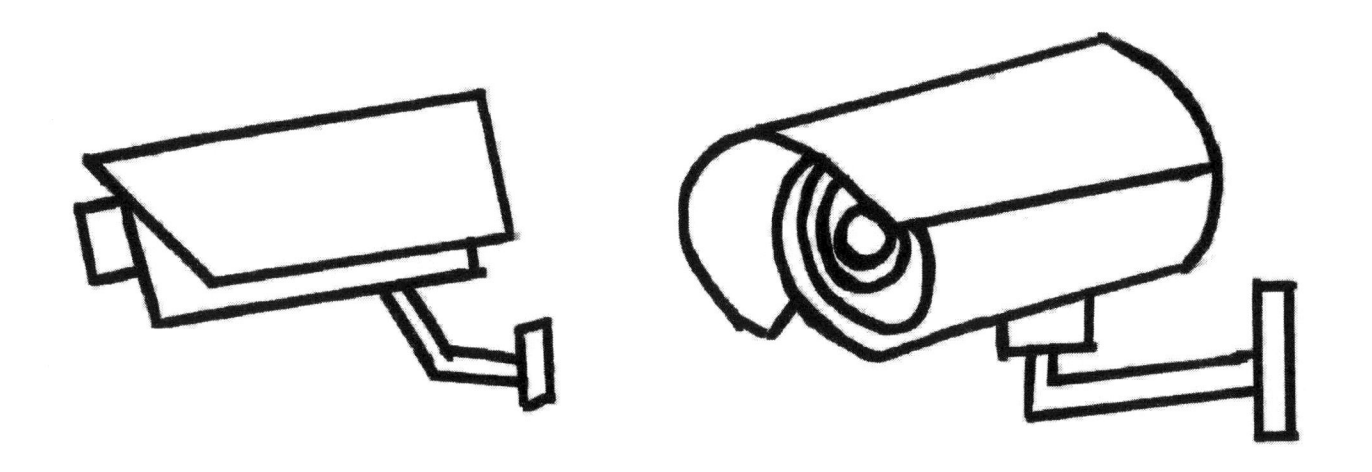

Can you draw a Camera?

Lewis Howard Latimer

Born: September 4, 1848, Chelsea, Massachusetts, U.S.
Died: December 11, 1928, Queens, New York City, U.S.
Major Inventions: evaporative air conditioner; improved process for manufacturing carbon filaments for light bulbs; improved toilet system for railroad cars.

Naissance : 4 Septembre, 1848, Chelsea, Massachusetts, U.S.
Décès : 11 Décembre 1928, Queens, New York City, U.S.
Inventions Majeures : climatiseur par évaporation; procédé amélioré de fabrication de filaments de carbone pour ampoules électriques ; système amélioré de toilettes pour les wagons de chemin de fer.

Can you draw a light bulb?

Alice H. Parker

Born: 1895, Morristown, New Jersey, U.S.
Died: 1920
Major Invention: central heating system that uses natural gas.

Naissance: 1895, Morristown, New Jersey, U.S.
Décès : 1920
Invention Majeure : Système de chauffage à gaz naturel.

GAS HEATING SYSTEM

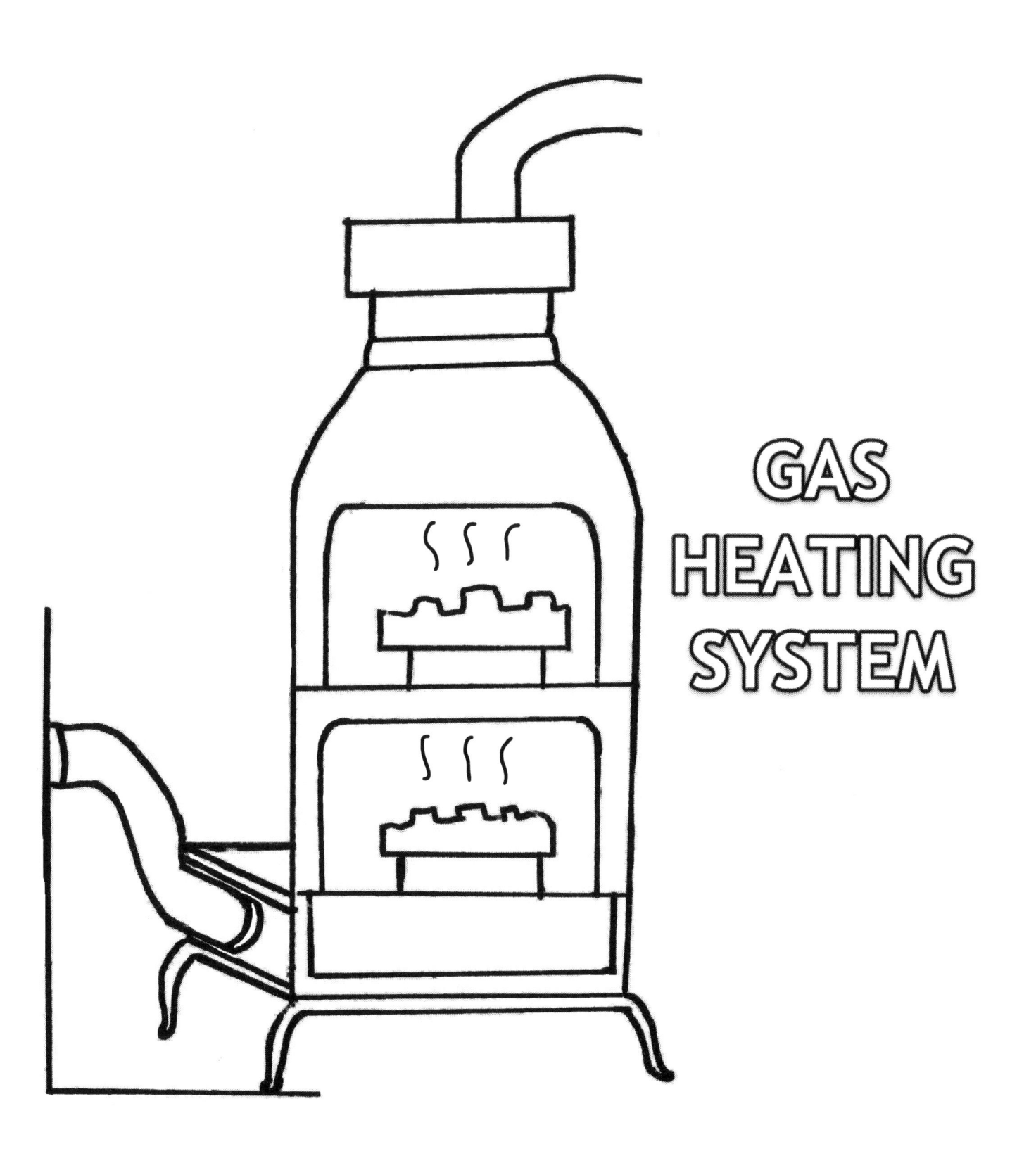

Granville Woods

Born: April 23, 1856, Columbus, Ohio, U.S.
Died: January 30, 1910, New York City, U.S.
Major Inventions: Synchronous Multiplex Railway Telegraph; Amusement Apparatus and Electric Railway Conduit; Improvement of Train Control and Braking Mechanisms

Naissance : 23 Avril 1856, Columbus, Ohio, U.S.
Décès: 30 Janvier 1910, New York City, U.S.
Inventions Majeures : Télégraphe ferroviaire multiplex synchrone ; Manèges pour divertissement ; Amélioration des mécanismes de contrôle et de freinage des trains.

Can you draw a railway?

Dr. Patricia E. Bath

Born: November 4, 1942, New York City, U.S.
Died: May 30, 2019, San Francisco, California, U.S.
Major Invention: device and technique for cataract surgery known as Laserphaco.

Naissance: 4 Novembre, 1942, New York City, U.S.
Décès: 30 Mai 2019, San Francisco, California, U.S.
Invention Majeure : Le Laserphaco et la technique pour opérer des cataractes.

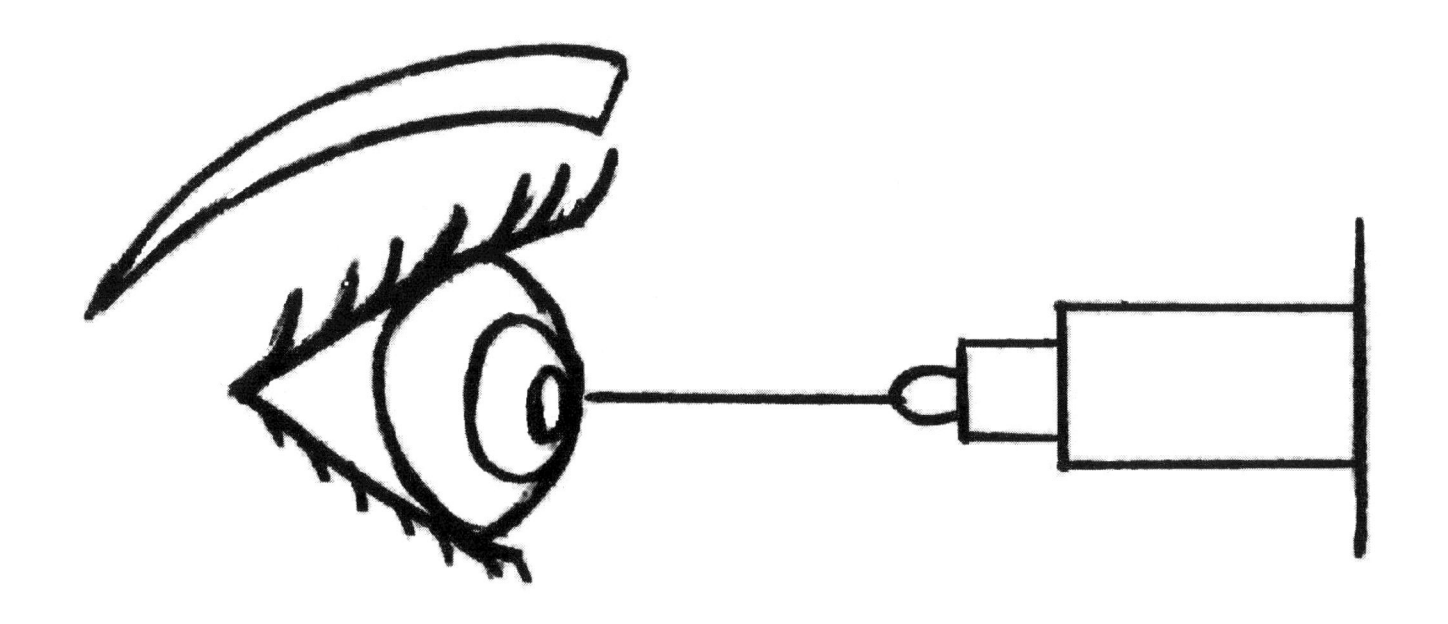

Can you draw an eye?

Percy Lavon Julian

Born: April 11, 1899, Montgomery, Alabama, U.S.
Died: April 19, 1975, Waukegan, Illinois, U.S.
Major Inventions: Synthetic cortisone, first synthesized the drug physostigmine to treat glaucoma, fire-extinguishing foam.

Naissance : 11 Avril, 1899, Montgomery, Alabama, U.S.
Décès : 19 Avril 1975, Waukegan, Illinois, U.S.
Inventions Majeures : Cortisone synthétique, La physostigmine synthétique pour le traitement du glaucome, de la mousse anti-incendie.

Can you draw a big fire?

Valerie Thomas

Born: February 8, 1943, Maryland, U.S.
Major Invention: 3D illusion transmitter.

Naissance : 8 Février 1943, Maryland, U.S.
Invention Majeure : transmetteur d'illusion d'images en 3D

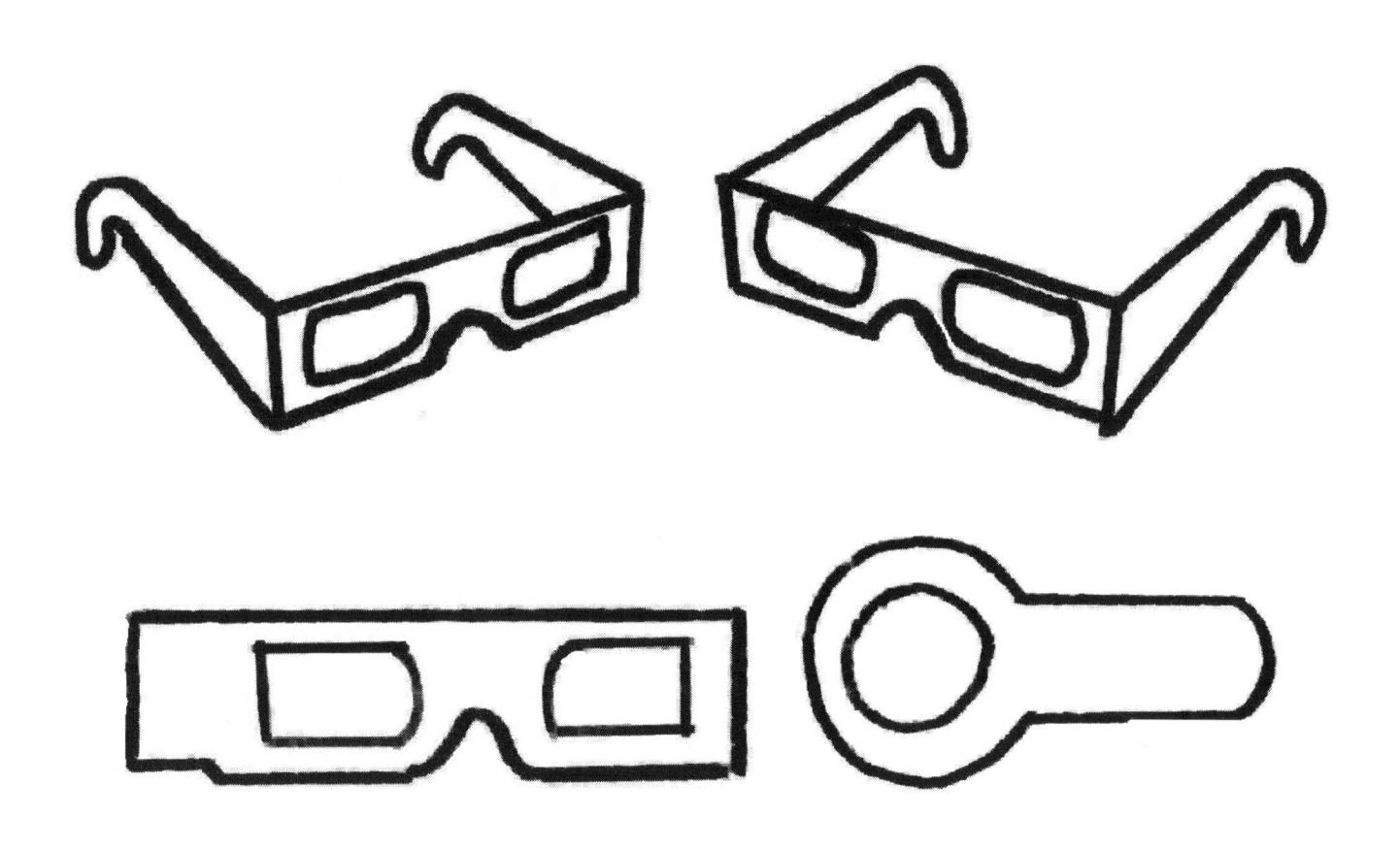

Can you draw 3D glasses?

Garrett Augustus Morgan

Born: March 4, 1877, Claysville, Harrison County, Kentucky, U.S.
Died: July 27, 1963, Cleveland, Ohio, U.S.
Major Inventions: Three signal traffic light, Gas mask

Naissance : 4 Mars, 1877, Claysville, Harrison County, Kentucky, U.S.
Décès : 27 Juillet 1963, Cleveland, Ohio, U.S.
Inventions Majeures : Feux de circulation à trois signaux, masque à gaz.

TRAFFIC SIGNAL

GAS MASK

Dr. Shirley Jackson, PHD

Born: August 5, 1946, Washington, D.C, U.S.
Major Invention: Caller ID.

Naissance : 5 Août 1946, Washington, D.C, U.S.
Invention Majeure : Identification des appels entrants.

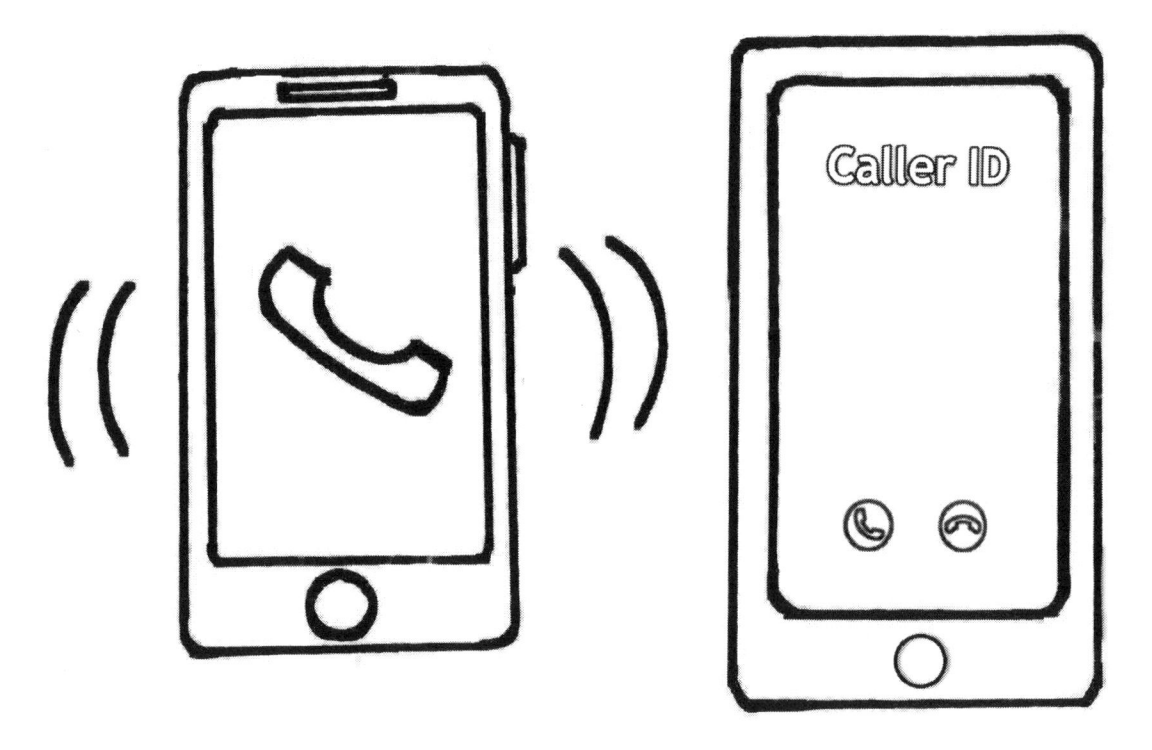

Can you draw the next superstar cellphone?

Alexander Miles

Born: May 18, 1838, Ohio, U.S.
Died: May 7, 1918, Seattle, Washington, U.S.
Major Invention: Improved Method for Automatic Opening and Closing Elevators doors.

Naissance : 18 Mai 1838, Ohio, U.S
Décès : 7 Mai 1918, Seattle, Washington, U.S.
Invention Majeure : Méthode d'ouverture et fermeture automatique des portes d'ascenseur.

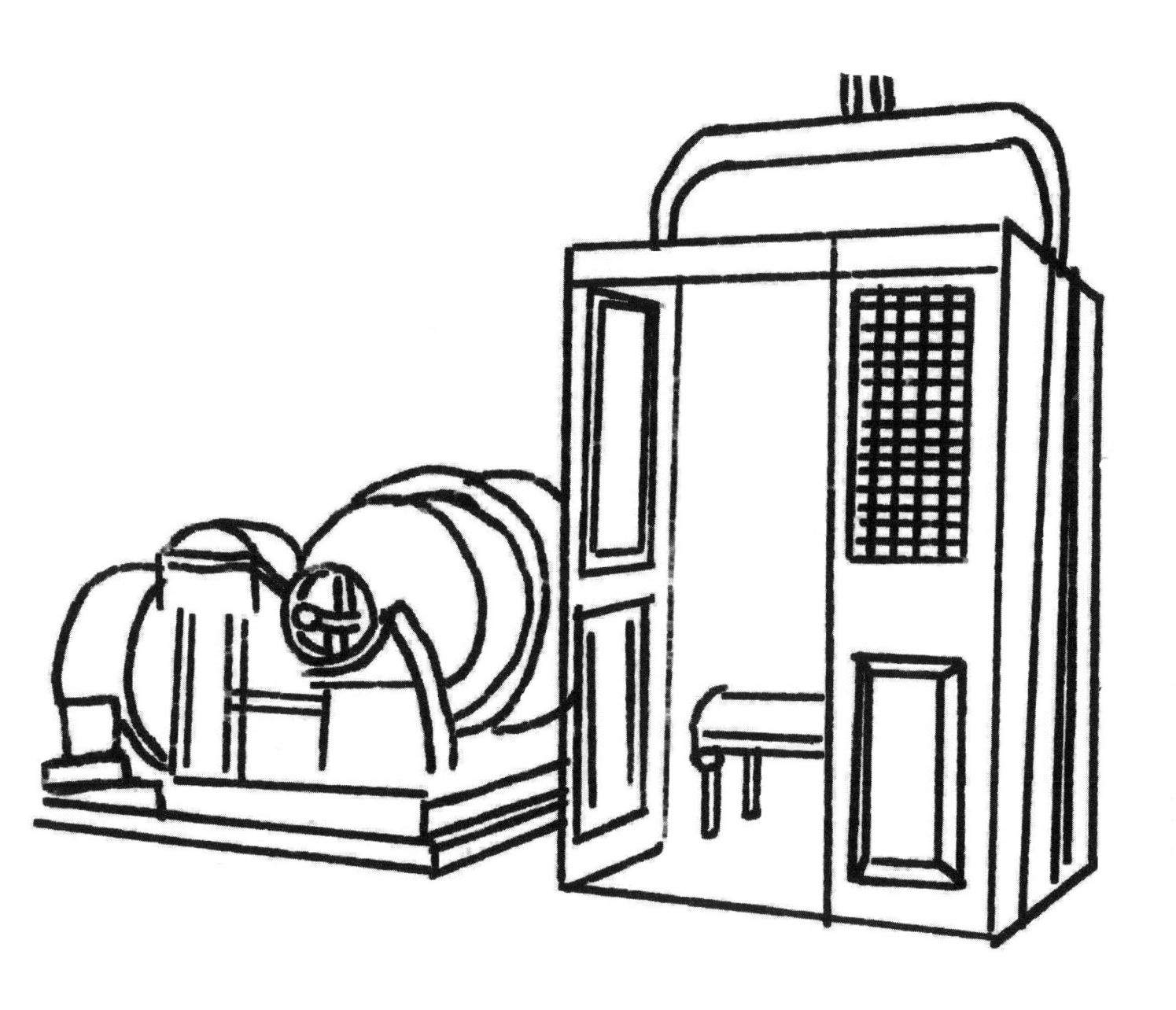

You are part of a project as an engineer. What should be the next improvement in elevators? Write it down here!

Dr. Gladys West, PHD

Born: Gladys Mae Brown, October 27, 1930, Sutherland, Virginia, U.S.
Major Invention: Basis model for the Global Positioning System (GPS).

Naissance : Née Gladys Mae Brown le 27 octobre 1930, Sutherland, Virginia, U.S.
Invention Majeure : Programme de base du GPS.

23

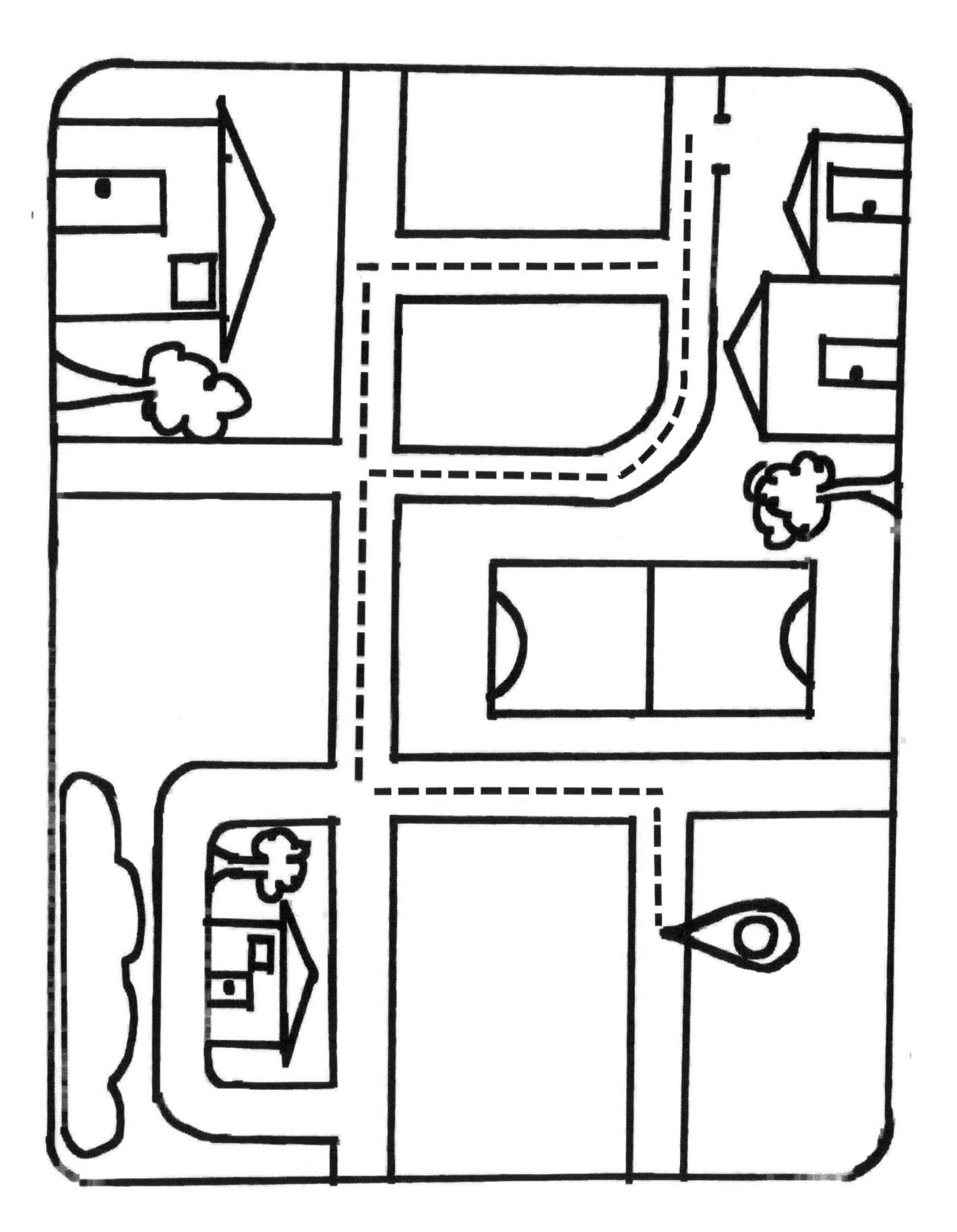

You are already thinking about you own invention, right? Can you draw it here? Use your skills and your imagination!

Made in the USA
Columbia, SC
05 February 2024